IN LOVING MEMORY OF

_____

MY PERSONAL JOURNEY
THROUGH GRIEF

_____

A JOURNEY WORTH TAKING:
GRIEVING WITH EASE

A JOURNEY WORTH TAKING: GRIEVING WITH EASE

KERRI BROOME

DEVINE SOUL ART
2019

A Journey Worth Taking:

Grieving with Ease

Copyright © 2019 by Kerri Broome.

All rights reserved.

This book or any portion thereof may not be reproduced or used in any manner whatsoever without the express written permission of the publisher except for the use of brief quotations in a book review or scholarly journal.

First Canadian Edition

First Printing: 2019

Book Design and Editing by Brandy Gagnon

ISBN 978-1-7770343-4-4

Devine Soul Art
1991 Foresters Falls Road Foresters Falls, ON K0J 1V0
www.devinesoulart.ca

DEDICATION

Jamie-
I never understood the importance of childhood memories and saying I love you, till the day you left us. I always admired your zest for life, your innocence and your childish way, how free you were in being yourself and the joy you brought to others. When you walked in a room your presence took over, your grand smile and your carefree way of being was contiguous. You touched many lives here in the physical and anyone who had the pleasure to meet or know you felt blessed to be a part of your journey. I will be forever grateful for you showing and guiding me along my path to connecting to my higher self, and most importantly pushing me to realize my gift isn't a hinderance it's a beautiful blessing that is to be shared and

offered to all that are willing to receive. I love you more than words could ever express. I am blessed to have had you in my life and continue a relationship that isn't understood yet by mankind, hopefully in time we will be able to have everyone understand and bless others with the beautiful and unique relationship between the spirit world and our linear fragments . I know you are proud of me and I thank you for giving me the gift of having pride in myself and the knowledge of knowing spirit is only ever a thought away.

Forever in my heart. Forever on my mind.

Love Kerri

IN LOVING MEMORY OF
JAMIE ERIC GUINDON

January 8, 1976 - January 21, 2011

CONTENTS

Introduction 1

Month One 3

Month Two 7

Month Three 11

Month Four 15

Month Five 19

Month Six 23

Month Seven 27

Month Eight 31

Month Nine 35

Month Ten 39

Month Eleven 43

Month Twelve 47

Month Thirteen 51

Month Fourteen 55

About the Author 63

x

ACKNOWLEDGEMENTS

With the most heartfelt sincerity I dedicate this book to my loving husband Rob. Thank you from the bottom of my heart for all your patience, kindness, and understanding while I find myself through this amazing journey called life. You have enhanced my life in so many ways, there are really no words to explain how much I deeply love you. I know that you do not understand completely how my gift works, and for that I love and respect you even more- you never complain about the long hours, the lingering smell of paint, and the extra-long honey-do list that I am always giving you. I realize how much time it takes away from our beautiful family. Your support and love have given me the opportunity and ability to explore my gifts and to be true to my true authentic self. I hope you know that every time you say, I love you and I respond to you "I know you do, that's the best part", I mean every word of that and then some. I couldn't have asked for a better life partner, more amazing father to our children and most importantly a best friend. I can't wait to see what we create in our future; I know it will be amazing because you will be right there with me. Thank you for being you and believing in me. I fall in love with you more and more each day.

All my love,

Kerri

INTRODUCTION

It's with the fullest heart I share with you,
my journey starts anew.
Remember me with joy and laughter,
while I look upon you from the hereafter.
Moment by moment- day by day,
I will be here to guide you along the way.
Take the time to sit still,
My presence is now your free will.
My soul now free to explore,
From the heavens above I am able to gaze down
and forever adore.

MONTH ONE

Loving me from a distance isn't going to be easy- always remember I am only ever a thought away.

Use this space to journal your most comforting memory about me.

MONTH TWO

I understand you are lonely,
I understand you are sad.
I understand you are heart broken,
I understand you are mad.
Please trust and know I am here,
I will never be far away.
When you think of me,
I will be right here beside you-
each and every day.
Each and every step along the way.

Use this space to journal one of your funniest memories about me.

MONTH THREE

Family is important.
I understand you are feeling blue but please
remember they need you too.

Use this space to create a mantra to repeat to yourself
whenever you start to feel overwhelmed by pain, regret,
guilt or despair.

MONTH FOUR

Your resilience is admirable. I am proud of you.

I understand this isn't easy for you- keep going you can do this. I am here for you.

Use this space to journal about a time your felt most connected to me.

MONTH FIVE

Always remember love has no boundaries-
it never dies.
My transition of energy is only a phase.
Energy never dies, it can only be transferred;
I am just vibrating on a different frequency.
My heart still belongs to you.
I loved you deeply while I was here,
I will continue to love you each and everyday. No matter
where you go, or what you do, I will support your
decisions and continue to love you.

Use this space to journal about who is in your support
system and why you can count on them.

MONTH SIX

I understand as time goes on you feel like
everyone around you has moved on.
Loneliness and heartache is extremely difficult.
Grief has many stages- you're doing amazing.
Go for a beautiful, long walk today.
I'll send you a sign that my presence
is with you.
Look for a dime, or perhaps a feather, or even an image in
the clouds- you may even get a glimpse of me from the
corner of your eye,
or a hint of my scent.
Please don't get discouraged if it doesn't
happen today; I promise when the time is right you will
feel my presence.

Use this space to journal about some of the things that you
feel have been helpful to you throughout your grieving
process.

MONTH SEVEN

I understand days are hard,
and nights are even harder.
Think of a time that we laughed and played, just before
you lay your head for a restful sleep.
I will see you in your dreams-
you may not remember but that's okay.
Trust that I am guiding you along the way.

Use this space to journal about the memory of me which
makes you smile the most.

MONTH EIGHT

As time goes on and you reminisce- think of our happy
days, think of the joy we gave each other-
always remember the good times.
Please don't dwell on the things that we didn't get to do,
or the hard times
that we may have endured.
All that matters is that you are ok.
Do something today that you always
wanted to do- I'll be right here beside you, cheering you
on and enjoying the
beautiful colours of your energy.
That helps my soul grow and brings
great peace to me.

Use this space to journal about a memory you have of me
which brings you great peace.

MONTH NINE

Don't forget to take a little timeout-
it's important that you take care of yourself.
I am so proud of you.
Keep going, you are doing great.
One step at a time.
They don't have to be big steps.
I love you.

Use this space to journal about ideas on ways you can honor me.

MONTH TEN

Sometimes we make plans for our life
which unfortunately change.
I am here to help guide you forward
throughout this rough time.
Things don't always go as planned- that we now
understand- and you need to
remember you are strong.
I admire your courage and your strength-
chin up. I am so proud of you.

Use this space to journal about things you can do to allow your feelings space to transform into something else.

MONTH ELEVEN

Some of the hardest things we endure
are blessings in disguise.
One day you will be able to help someone else with their process of grief. That day I will shine down on you with pride and joy.
I love you dearly, you're a beautiful soul, and have so much to offer others.
Help someone in need.
Compassion, understanding, and experience make for the greatest teachers.
Shine your light bright.
Go forward with love and a full heart.
I'll be with you cheering you on as
your biggest fan. I am grateful for you.

Use this space to journal about memories of me which you feel grateful to have.

MONTH TWELVE

Don't forget to take some time
with your friends- go for a walk or read a book. Self-
rejuvenating is important.
Pamper yourself today!
It's okay- you deserve it.
A little time out never hurt anyone, and it's not selfish to
do good things for yourself!
Be kind to yourself you've been through a lot the last little
while, you need a little pampering.
I am here for you.

Use this space to journal about things you are willing to try
to be more compassionate towards yourself.

MONTH THIRTEEN

Perhaps I didn't say I love you enough- and whether I did
or didn't, please know that
I loved you the best way I knew how.
Now that my soul is free, I want you to
understand that I love you more and more each day.
Enough time has passed now since I've
transitioned- my life review is now complete.
I now understand each and every interaction and
encounter that my soul energy participated in.
I understand unconditional love completely
and that's what I carry for you.
For when I did my review, I was able to see and
experience each and every encounter that I had through
the soul eyes of the people that I was blessed to have had
time and interaction with.
I have no regrets, only growth.
I thank you for being part of my journey that was worth
taking because you were such
a precious part of my life.
Our relationship will only flourish from here on out.

Use this space to journal our most meaningful
conversation, or a time I gave your great advice.

MONTH FOURTEEN

Please trust in me that our relationship through source energy is much more unique and beautiful then the human experience of relationships.
In human life we have obligations, we have jobs, and things that keep us from being
apart from each other.
Now that my soul has returned to pure source energy, understand there is nothing holding me back from connecting with you on my part.
Please do not fear my presence for I would never harm you.
I know that you will never forget me.
My wish for you is to find happiness, joy, and peace. Take the time to experience new adventures-love and live your life to the fullest.
Always remember when making decisions that I will always and only ever want what is best for you.
I will be with you no matter where you go or what you do. Practice your free will and enjoy all that life has to offer you, when it's your day to return home I will be there waiting for you with open arms.

Use this space to journal about a time when I made your feel loved.

Loving you yesterday, today, and tomorrow.

ABOUT THE AUTHOR

Kerri Broome was born in the rural town of Arnprior, Ontario in 1974. She is an extraordinarily gifted healer of mind, body, and soul.

www.ingramcontent.com/pod-product-compliance
Lightning Source LLC
Chambersburg PA
CBHW071228160426
43196CB00012B/2445